The Urbana Free Library

To renew materials call
217-367-4057

Why Don't Gorillas Lay Eggs?

By Katherine Smith

Consultant: Nicola Davies

WATERBIRD BOOKS

Columbus, Ohio

9-05
13-00

Mc Graw Hill **Children's Publishing**

This edition published in the United States of America in 2004 by
Waterbird Books
an imprint of McGraw-Hill Children's Publishing,
a Division of The McGraw-Hill Companies
8787 Orion Place
Columbus, Ohio 43240-4027

www.MHkids.com

Library of Congress Cataloging-in-Publication Data is on file with the publisher.

First published in Great Britain in 2004 by *ticktock* Media Ltd.,
Unit 2, Orchard Business Centre, North Farm Road, Tunbridge Wells, Kent TN3 3XF.
Text and illustrations © 2004 *ticktock* Entertainment Ltd.
We would like to thank: Meme Ltd. and Elizabeth Wiggans.
Every effort has been made to trace the copyright holders, and we apologize in advance for any unintentional omissions.
We would be pleased to insert the appropriate acknowledgements in any subsequent edition of this publication.

Printed in China

1-57768-949-6

1 2 3 4 5 6 7 8 9 10 TTM 09 08 07 06 05 04

The **McGraw·Hill** Companies

CONTENTS

Any words appearing in the text in bold, **like this**, are explained in the Glossary.

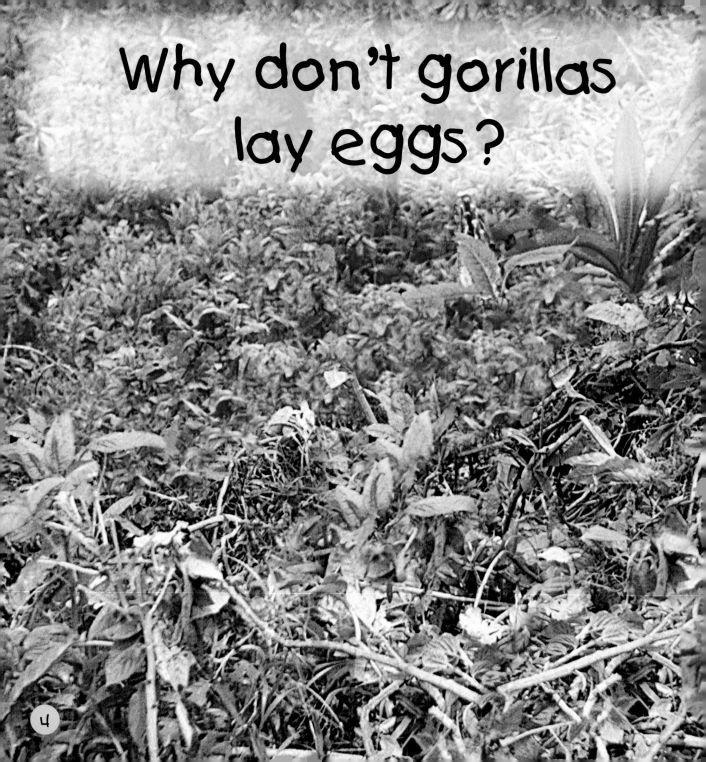

Why don't gorillas
lay eggs?

Because gorillas are mammals. Like most mammals, they give birth to live babies.

Like human babies, baby gorillas need a lot of care from their mothers. They stay with their mothers for many years until they learn to take care of themselves.

The baby gorilla feeds on its mother's milk.

Baby gorillas start to crawl when they are six months old. They can walk by the time they are three years old.

6

Gorillas usually have just one baby at a time.

Young male gorillas leave their family groups when they are about 11 years old to build nests of their own.

Mothers carry their young to keep them safe from danger.

Why don't gorillas have long tails?

Because gorillas are apes, not monkeys.

Only monkeys have tails. Gorillas belong to the great ape family, along with orang-utans, chimpanzees, and gibbons. Instead of long tails, apes use their long arms and their hands and feet to reach out and grab hold of things.

Researchers think that gorillas have very good eyesight.

Orang-utans are the only great apes that don't live in groups.

Like all apes, gorillas can reason.
They can work out solutions to problems.

Gorillas' arms are longer than their legs.

Why don't gorillas have colorful coats?

Because gorillas' coats allow them to blend in with their surroundings.

A gorilla's coat acts as **camouflage**, allowing the gorilla to blend in with its surroundings. The gorilla is hard to spot in the **rain forest**.

Gorillas have no hair on their chest, palms, nose, ears, lips, or on the soles of their feet.

Mountain gorillas live in cold mountain forests. They have thicker coats to keep them warm.

Baby gorillas have white tufts of fur on their bottoms. Researchers think that this helps their mothers find them in the rain forest.

Why don't gorillas live on their own?

Because gorillas are very sociable animals.

Female gorillas and their young live, eat, play, travel, and sleep in groups called **harems**. Each group has one male leader called a **silverback**. He alerts the group when there is danger.

Adult males have silver patches of fur on their backs. This is where they get the name "silverback."

When danger threatens, the silverback roars, screams, beats its chest, and charges at its enemies.

18

The silverback is twice as big as a female gorilla.

Gorillas frequently groom one another. Grooming helps gorillas stay free of fleas and other parasites.

Why don't gorillas get wet when it rains?

Because gorillas build their own shelters.

Just like human beings, gorillas avoid going out in the rain. They bend branches and leaves down over their heads to make a shelter.

Gorillas use their fingers and toes to pick things up and to build shelters.

Every day, gorillas build nests of fresh grass and leaves. They sleep in the nests at night.

Gorillas' fur is not waterproof, but their fur does protect them from the cold.

Why don't gorillas eat hamburgers?

Because gorillas are herbivores. They don't eat meat.

Gorillas eat fruit, shoots, roots, tree bark, and leaves. They spend a lot of time eating. Eating frequently gives them the energy they need.

Gorillas do not need to drink water because they get water from the fruit and leaves they eat.

Gorillas are mostly herbivores, but occasionally eat grubs and **termites**.

Gorillas can grip with their hands. This allows them to pick up food.

Gorillas help make the forest grow. Their droppings contain the plant seeds they have eaten.

27

Gorilla PROFILE

Life span

Up to 35 years.

Size

5 feet 9 inches. That is about as tall as a male human being!

Weight

Up to 359 pounds. That is twice as heavy as a male human being!

Numbers

There are an estimated 50,000 gorillas living in the wild.

28

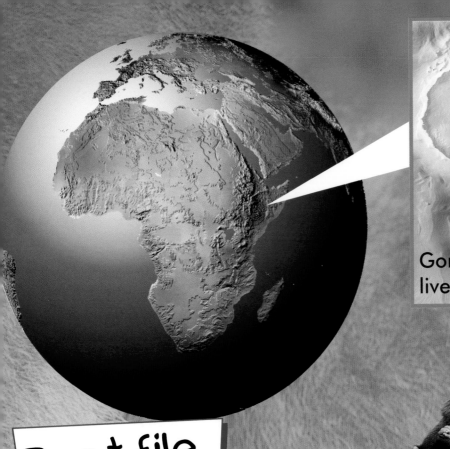

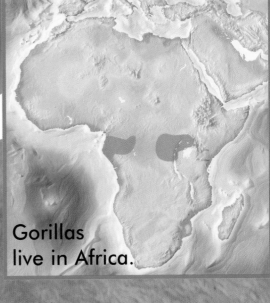

Gorillas live in Africa.

Fact file

There are five different types of gorilla:

- The **mountain** gorilla
- The **Bwindi Forest** gorilla
- The **eastern lowland** gorilla
- The **western lowland** gorilla
- The **Cross River** gorilla

Gorillas are an **endangered species**. Because they are hunted and have lost their habitat, there are only 650 mountain gorillas left in the world.

Gorillas are peaceful animals but will attack if they are threatened.

29

GLOSSARY

Ape

An animal such as a chimpanzee or gorilla that is closely related to human beings and has no tail.

Camouflage

Colorings or markings on an animal or insect that allows it to blend in with its natural surroundings.

Endangered species

A species of animal that is in danger of extinction (dying out) because it is being hunted by humans or it is losing its habitat.

Harem

The name for a group of female gorillas.

Herbivore	An animal that does not eat meat.
Mammals	Animals that are warm-blooded and produce milk for their young.
Rain forest	A thick, bushy forest in a tropical area that has an annual rainfall of at least 100 inches.
Silverback	An adult male gorilla that is in charge of a harem. It has a silver patch of fur on its back.
Termites	Small antlike insects found in hot, rainy areas.

INDEX